The Lasting Legacy of the Ancient Roman Civilization

Ancient History Books for Kids
Children's Ancient History

BABY PROFESSOR

EDUCATION KIDS

Speedy Publishing LLC

40 E. Main St. #1156

Newark, DE 19711

www.speedypublishing.com

Copyright 2017

The great Roman Empire came to an end in Western Europe before 500 C.E., over 1500 years ago. Its armies are long gone, as are its emperors. What remains? What did we inherit from Rome? Read on and find out!

A Roman Legacy

The "legacy" we inherit from the Roman Empire is both physical and in ideas and traditions. During the time of the Republic and the Empire, Rome developed a wide range of innovations, ways of solving problems, and ways of communicating that we still rely on today. The very word we use for an organized body of people with a common culture is a "civilization", and "civilization" comes from the Latin word for city, civitas. Rome, the capital and mother of the Empire, was the prime city of all Rome's citizens.

ΣΩΤΗΡΙ
ΛΜΙΝΙΚΙΟΣΝΑΤΑΛΙΟΣ
ΥΠΑΤΟΣΑΝΘΥΠΑΤΟΣΛΒΥΗΣ
ΑΥΓΟΥΡ·ΠΡΕΣΒΕΥΤΗΣ·ΚΑΙ
ΑΝΤΙΣΤΡΑΤΗΓΟΣ·ΣΕΒΑΣΤΟΥ
ΜΥΣΙΑΣΤΗΣ ΚΑΤΩ
ΤΟΝΝΑΟΝΚΑΙΤΟΝΒΩΜΟΝ
ΑΝΕΘΗΚΕΝ

Let's look at a few of the treasures in our legacy from Rome!

Our Writing Style

In Europe and North America, most writing uses one of three scripts: Latin, Cyrillic, and Greek. All three are children of the writing style the Roman Empire used. Latin script, writing in the Latin alphabet that the Romans developed from what they themselves inherited from the Greeks, Phoenicians, and Etruscans, is the way of writing used more than any other all around the world.

The Greek alphabet became the main writing mode of the Eastern Roman Empire, from 500 to 1500 C.E., and is still in use in the Greek-speaking world. The Cyrillic alphabet carries Slavic languages like Russian, Ukrainian, and many others.

ΑΝΔΡΟΝ

ΚΑΙΠΡΟΤ

ΙΟΝΟΣΑ

ΘΑΡΤΟΝΟ

I

TITYRE TU PATULE RECUBANS SUB TEGMINE FAG

SILVESTREM TENUI MUSAM MEDITARIS AVENA

NOS PATRIAE FINES ET DULCIA LINQUIMUS ARVA

NOS PATRIAM FUGIMUS TU TITYRE LENTUS IN UMBRA

FORMOSAM RESONARE DOCES AMARYLLIDA SILVAS

O MELIBOEE DEUS NOBIS HAEC OTIA FECIT

NAMQUE ERIT ILLE MIHI SEMPER DEUS ILLIUS ARAM

SAEPE TENER NOSTRIS AB OVILIBUS IMBUET AGNUS

ILLE MEAS ERRARE BOVES UT CERNIS ET IPSUM

Literature

In Europe from the fall of the western Roman Empire in the fifth century until well into the Enlightenment in the 16th century, most scholars, scientists, and politicians wrote their important documents in Latin. Roman authors, from historians like Tacitus and Julius Caesar to poets like Pindar and Virgil, were hugely popular throughout Europe and gave writers a standard and example to work toward.

In the 10th century, a Saxon nun wanted to create a form of entertainment that could also deliver Christian teaching. She took the Roman slapstick comedies of Plautus and Terence as her models, and wrote plays that were the first seeds of European theater in France, Germany, and England.

William Shakespeare

William Shakespeare drew directly from the writers of the Roman Empire for the plots of some of his comedies and dramas, and for the details of plays like Julius Caesar and Antony and Cleopatra.

Measuring Days and Years

The calendar we use today is based on the Julian calendar that Julius Caesar introduced. For the Romans, the first months of the year were Ianuarius, Februarius, and Martius. Does that sound familiar?

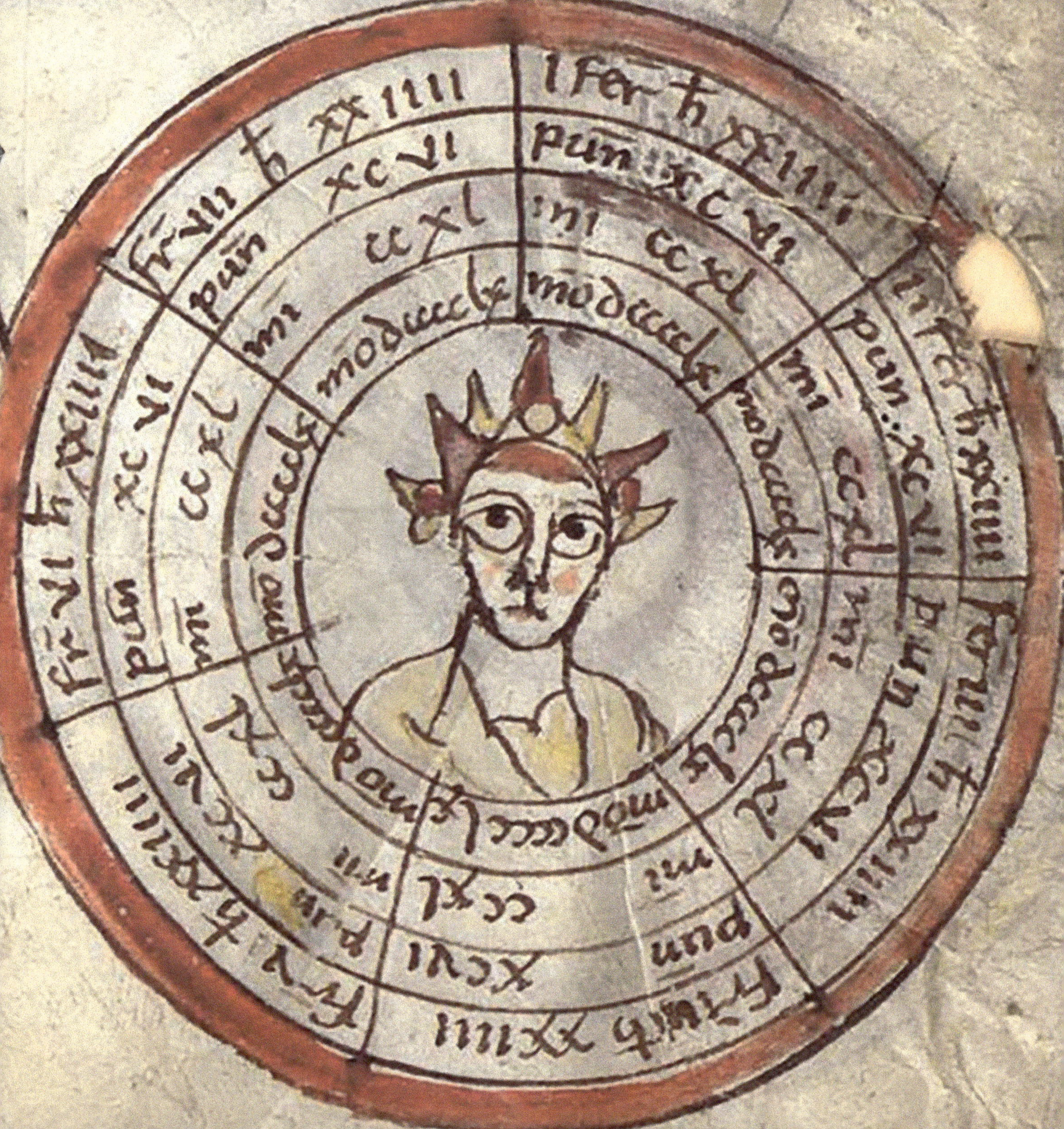
I fer h xxiiii
pun xcvi
ini ccxl
modcccclx

Our seven-day week is based on a Roman system. The Romans knew of seven heavenly bodies besides the Earth: the Sun, the Moon, Mercury, Venus, Mars, Saturn and Jupiter. They named each day of the week after one of the heavenly bodies that they thought influenced that day, and various modern languages retain the names. In English, Saturday is "the day of Saturn"; in French, Tuesday, or mardi, is "the day of Mars".

Philosophy, Religion and Science

The Roman Empire preserved and passed on scientific, religious, and philosophical thought from Greece, Babylon, and Egypt, and made additions of its own. Roman philosophers like Marcus Aurelius and Epictetus have continued to influence modern thought.

Marcus Aurelius

Christian theologians like Augustine of Hippo brought together pre-Christian ideas from thinkers like Plato with the wisdom of the Bible, and greatly enriched Christianity as it spread and became the major religion of western Europe and the New World.

Galen, who was a Greek physician under the Roman Empire, wrote essays and studies on medicine that were influential for centuries. The scholar Ptolemy developed a theory of astronomy and the solar system that was the accepted model until (and after!) the time of Renaissance thinkers like Galileo and Copernicus.

Galen

Law and Politics

After the Roman Empire fell, new states that emerged had to develop systems of government and law. Many of those systems are based on Roman legal and political ideas. In modern courts, many procedures, required documents, and offices still have their Latin tags—for instance, if you don't have a lawyer and are defending yourself in a trial, in court language you are "appearing pro se", which means exactly the same thing but sounds more elegant.

The basic pattern of many trials, where each side in a dispute has an attorney who speaks and argues, a judge who keeps order, and a jury that considers the evidence and brings in a verdict of guilty or not guilty, is based on what developed in the Roman world.

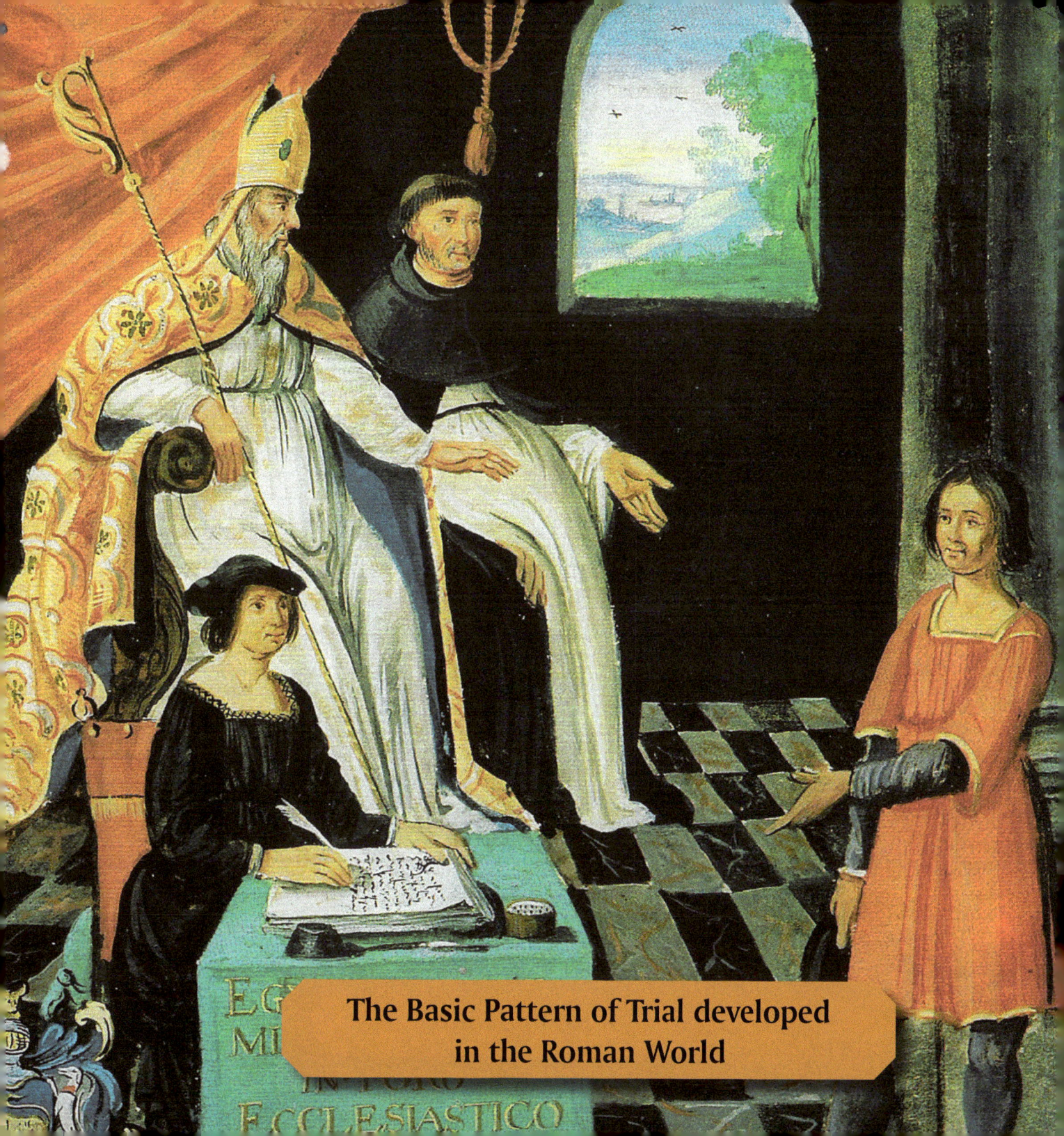

The Basic Pattern of Trial developed in the Roman World

EG
MI
IN FORO
ECCLESIASTICO

Roman Senate

Most modern countries that call themselves democracies or republics base some or all of their structures on concepts developed during the Roman Republic. After seven kings in the years after its founding, Rome moved to a representative democracy where the leaders "govern with the consent of the governed". This principle underlies democratic elections and bodies like the British House of Commons and the U.S. House of Representatives.

On the other hand, the U.S. Senate and the British House of Lords continue the Roman concept of the "Senate", the body of wealthy, powerful, and influential people who might have a different idea about what is good government from what the general public wants.

British House of Lords

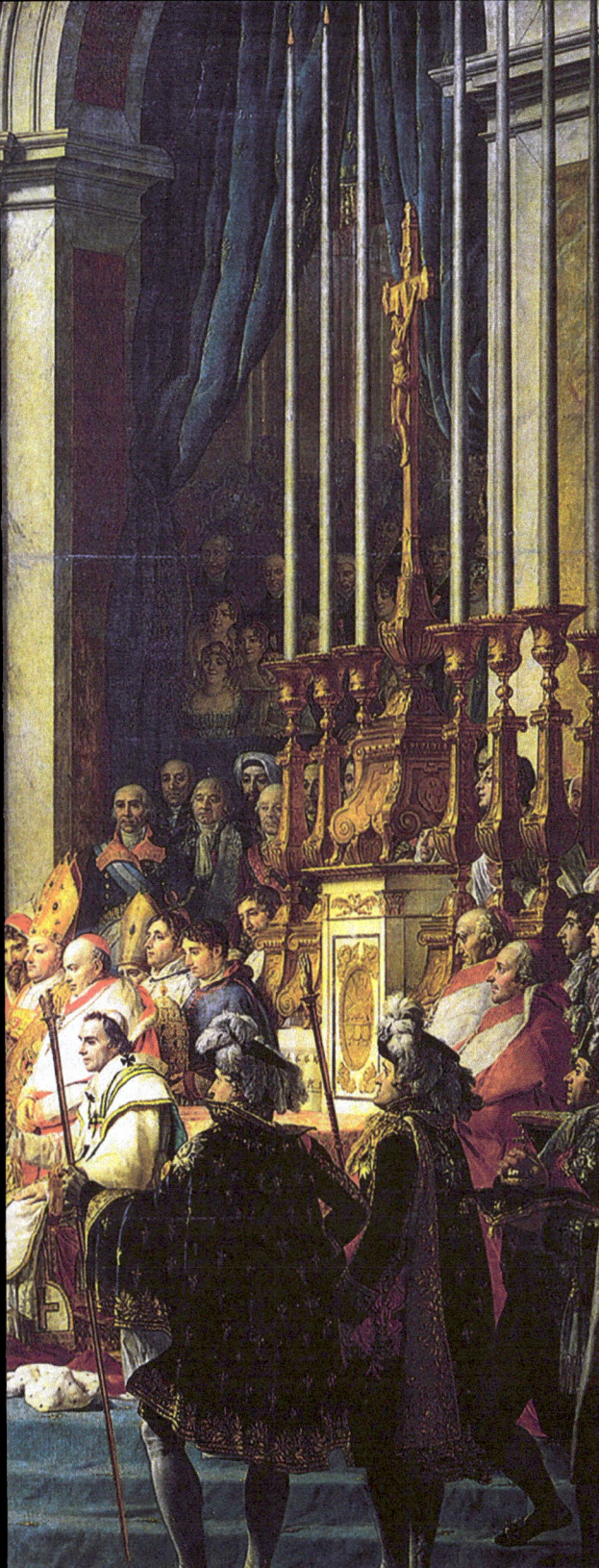

Between the fall of the Roman Empire and the rise of democratic government, most states had a king as the ruler. The king often tried to claim the authority of the Roman tradition to strengthen his position and power. In Germany, the kings were called Kaisers, a name derived from Caesar. In Russia, the supreme ruler was the Czar, which also comes from Caesar.

After the western Roman Empire fell in the fifth century, the Eastern Roman Empire, based in what is now Istanbul in Turkey, continued for another thousand years (read the Baby Professor book, The Byzantine Empire, to learn more about the Eastern Empire). The Eastern Empire always considered itself the true continuation of Rome. When it fell, part of it became what is now the nation of Romania—the "land of the Romans", even though it is hundreds of miles away from Rome!

Eastern Roman Empire

Roads and Cities

As the Roman Republic and Empire spread across Europe, North Africa, and the Middle East, it strengthened its control over new provinces by establishing colonia, colony cities. Many of these colonia continued after the fall of Rome and now are among the world's great cities: Munich, Paris, London, Marseilles, and many others.

The Romans connected these cities to each other, to trading ports, and to other parts of the Empire by over 300,000 miles of roads. Over 50,000 miles of these roads were paved with stone to make travel easy in most weather and for armies, traders, pilgrims, and tourists. Many of those roads have new lives in the modern world as high-speed highways; you can find the remains of many others all through Western Europe.

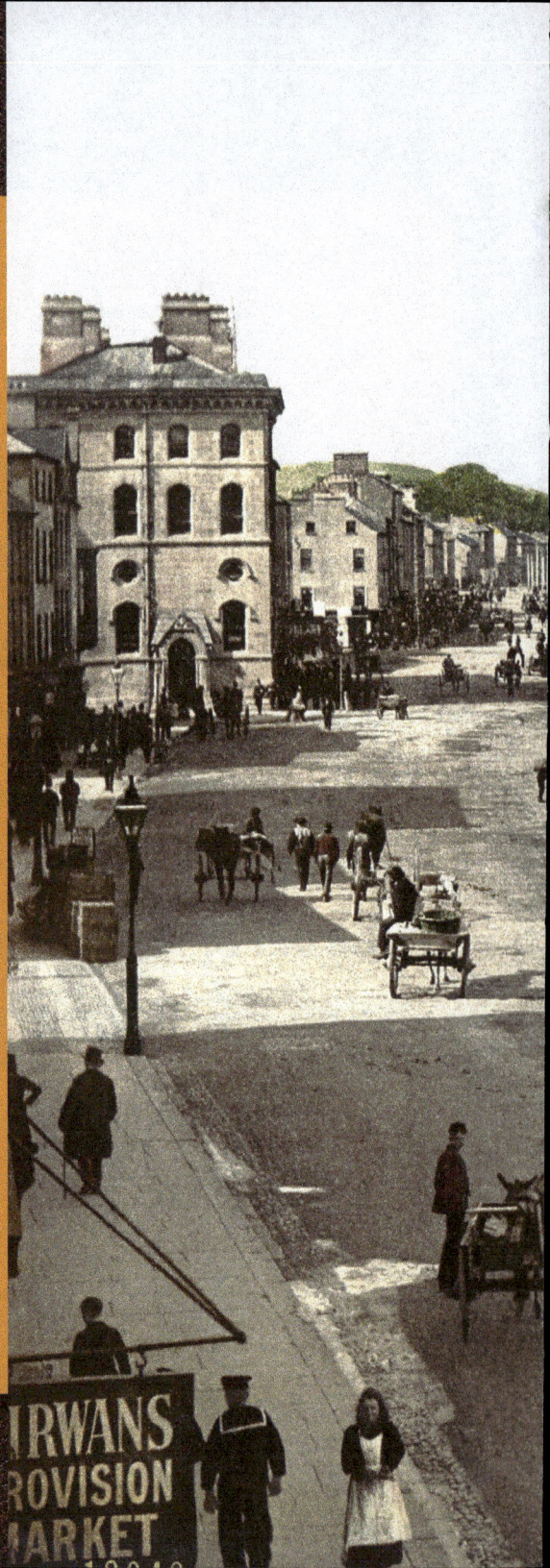

When architects want to create a building that looks confident, permanent, and reliable, they often copy elements of buildings the Romans put up 2,000 years ago.

Architecture

We can still see all over Europe and the Middle East the remains of great buildings and other structures from the Roman Empire. These include arches and columns that once were part of great buildings and temples, the ruins of amphitheaters where gladiators fought and chariot races took place, aqueducts to carry fresh water to the cities, and domes over large open spaces in buildings.

Ruins of Amphitheaters

Trading Port

Ancient Roman Aqueducts

The Romans developed and invented concrete, mortar and cement, some of which is still holding buildings and aqueducts together today.

The Romans developed under-floor heating and central heating for their houses. They had huge, heated public baths which were available for all citizens. They created open spaces where people could meet, and established a tradition of putting up statues of great heroes, or of the gods, in those spaces.

Living

The way we live now owes a lot to the way the Romans lived then. Here are some simple examples:

Three-course Meal

The Romans developed the style of a formal or family meal that has an introductory course, a main course, and a dessert.

Wine-making and Wine-tasting

Romans developed strains of grapes that yielded sweet juice that could be fermented into tasty wine. This tradition continues all through parts of the world that were part of the Empire.

Mass Entertainment

When you go to the stadium to see a football game, or to the outdoor venue for a rock concert, you are continuing the tradition of mass entertainment that became established throughout the Roman Empire. When you turn out for a parade with marching bands, soldiers, people throwing trinkets and candies, and dancers and clowns, you are following a tradition the Romans started for their annual holidays.

The Romans provided these events for free, as a way of keeping the city population content, and as part of great national celebrations.

We Inherit From the Past

The days of the Roman Empire are far behind us, but in some ways, what Rome developed still influences our modern world. Read more Bay Professor books about our past, like The Role Families Play in Roman Culture and Society and The Battles of Rome, to learn more about how our present came to be.